Sleeping in a Sack

Camping Activities for Kids

Linda White

Illustrated by Fran Lee

GIBBS·SMITH
PUBLISHER

Salt Lake City

For my father, whose love of camping lives on in his children
and grandchildren. - L.W.

For my dad, A. William Lee, who encouraged me to be brave—
and when you go camping you have to be brave. - F.L.

First edition
02 01 00 99 98 5 4 3 2 1

Text copyright © 1998 by Linda White
Illustration copyright © 1998 by Fran Lee

This is a Gibbs Smith Junior Book, published by
Gibbs Smith, Publisher
P.O. Box 667
Layton, Utah 84041

Design by Fran Lee & Janice Jenkins
Printed and bound in China

Note: Some of the activities suggested in this book require adult assistance and supervision, as noted throughout. The publisher and author assume no responsibility for any damages or injuries incurred while performing any of the activities in this book.

Library of Congress Cataloging-in-Publication Data

White, Linda, 1948-
Sleeping in a sack: camping activities for kids / Linda White:
illustrations by Fran Lee. 1st ed.
p. cm.
Summary: An introduction to camping, including the type of gear needed, safety tips, activities, games,
songs, and recipes.
ISBN 0-87905-830-7
1. Camping — Juvenile literature. 2. Family recreation —Juvenile literature. (1. Camping.)
I. Lee, Fran, ill. II. Title.
GV191.7.W48 1998
796.54'5—dc21   97-3093
                                                                            CIP
                                                                            AC

contents

Living Outdoors	4	No-Utensil Cooking	31
Types of Camping	6	Recipes	33
Choosing Outdoor Gear	7	**Camp Skills and Pleasures**	42
Shelter Stuff	7	Knotty Campers	42
Necessary Camp Stuff	12	Cutting-edge Safety	44
Cooking and Eating Stuff	14	Nature Watch	46
Cleanup Stuff	16	First Aid	48
Clothing Stuff	18	Staying Found	49
Planning Your Trip	20	Look at Those Stars!	52
Selecting a Campsite	22	Singing 'Round the Ol' Campfire	55
Setting Up Camp	23	Games Campers Play	57
Cooking Area	23	Fun After Dark	59
Sleeping Area	24		
Backwoods Plumbing	25	**Green Camping**	62
Camp Chow	28	**Packing List**	63
Campfires	29	**For More Information**	64

Living outdoors

What are you going to do this weekend? Watch TV, play video games, clean your room? Would you rather sing songs around a blazing campfire, roast marshmallows on a stick until they are gooey, and sleep in a sack under the stars? Then you should try camping.

Getting started in the world of camping can be confusing. Outdoor shops offer oodles of choices in equipment and gadgets. Fortunately, you don't have to buy everything you see there. Much of what you need you probably already have. Add a few basics—mainly a tent and a sleeping bag—learn a few camp skills, and you'll be ready to head for the woods.

The best camping trips are well-planned ones. It's no fun to be miles from any town, have the wood laid for your campfire, your hot dogs on a stick, only to find out you've forgotten to bring matches. There'll be a cold and hungry night ahead.

This book will help you organize a great trip. You'll learn what to look for when choosing camp equipment; what food, clothes, and tools

to pack; how to choose and set up a camp home; and some games, songs, and crafts to keep you entertained while you're living in the wild. You'll find Rikki Raccoon along the trail to share camp secrets and offer tried-and-true tips.

Having an adult camp with you is a must. You'll be going places you haven't been before, doing new things, and using unfamiliar tools. You'll want your adult to help you purchase gear, set up camp, know when it's safe to build a campfire, and many other things. Besides, it's always more fun to do things together.

When you see this symbol ▬▬▬ , the use of something sharp, such as a knife, ax, or camp saw, is required. This symbol 🔥 alerts you to a burn hazard. Make sure to ask your adult for help with each of those tasks.

Can you smell the wood smoke? Ready to hear the night music of the out-of-doors? Let's go camping!

types of camping

Whether you live in a high-rise apartment or a secluded farm, your first camping trip may be in your own back-yard, back porch, or balcony. For that kind of backyard camping, your equip-ment might be a tarp for a tent, blankets for a sleeping bag, and a flashlight. Grub can be cooked on the barbecue grill.

Backpackers carry their equipment into the backwoods on their backs. They take only what they absolutely have to have: a compact tent, a sleeping bag, a backpacker's stove, a cooking pot, some dried food, a change of clothes, and some drinking water.

Car campers can take more of the comforts of home: a bigger tent, pillows to go with the sleeping bags, a more elaborate cooking setup, some folding chairs to sit on, games, fishing gear, and even a double-jointed teddy bear.

Campers on extended trips prefer larger tents for the extra room, cots for a more comfortable night's sleep, and often a small kitchen cabinet to keep the needed food and cooking utensils.

(choosing outdoor gear ☆

Backpacking tent

← rain fly

The kind of camping you do, where you camp, and how long you stay determines what you take. Different campgrounds, whether perched beside shining seas, in tall grasses, or on mountaintops, offer different facilities. Some have showers and flush toilets. Primitive campgrounds may not even have a metal ring to hold your campfire, and you'll have to dig a pit for a toilet. Libraries and bookstores have books that can tell what facilities each campground has and maps to show you how to get there.

The time of year you camp also changes the gear you take. Summer campers often strap bicycles on top of their cars before they head out. Winter campers build snow caves and snuggle in below the howling winds and deep snows. They leave the tent at home and pack extra-warm clothes and sleeping bags. It's important that you check the weather forecast for the place you're heading so you can plan ahead.

Let's take a look at what you need, starting with the big stuff.

Shelter Stuff

Tents

You'll miss a real treat if you don't sleep out where you can count the stars. But since the weather can change suddenly, a tent, your portable house, is desirable for most trips. It'll keep the rain out of your face and the mosquitoes out of your ears. It'll also give you a private place to change clothes.

- Backpacking tents, used by campers hiking deep into the backcountry, hold one or two campers in close quarters and may weigh as little as five or six pounds. Good ones can cost several hundred dollars.

Dome tent

- Dome tents, shaped like a turtle shell, can be a good choice for a small family or a few friends. They are easy to set up, sturdy, and come in a range of prices (and qualities). But watch out: when the tag says the tent sleeps three, that may not include room even for the next day's clothes.

Cabin-style tent

- Larger, cabin-style tents, made like a cloth building with walls and a roof, are great choices for big groups and people on longer outings. The extra space and stand-up headroom really make a difference.

Whatever size and style you choose, the most important function of the tent is to keep you dry. A rain fly will direct moisture away from the tent. A sheet of heavyweight plastic spread under the tent, called a ground cloth, will keep the floor dry and clean. Buy it by the yard at hardware, home, and garden stores.

When choosing a tent, look for:
- a rain fly
- two layers of fabric in places where poles or ropes will attach
- heavy-duty, double-stitched seams
- screens to keep out crawling, flying, and buzzing critters
- a small porch for storage or sitting
- room for relaxing, playing games, or reading on rainy days.

CRAFTY CAMPER: TENT

Eventually you'll want a manufactured tent because of its useful features, but you can make your own tent for clear, warm nights.

1. Find two trees about ten feet apart.
2. Tie a rope to the two trees about four feet from the ground. The rope should be tight so it doesn't sag.
3. Throw a tarp or old blanket over the rope so that half of the material hangs on either side of the rope.
4. Using tent stakes (available at outdoor shops) or pegs made from branches, stake the four corners to the ground. Add another stake between the corners on each side.

Sleeping Bags

The tent will keep you dry but it won't keep you warm. That's the job of your camp bed, the sleeping bag. Sleep sacks come in two basic styles—rectangular and mummy. Many campers consider the rectangular bag more comfortable. It's roomy enough to give some wiggle room. Some rectangular bags have two top flaps, one light and one heavy. By adding or tossing them off as the temperature changes, you will find your sleeping bag not too hot, not too cold, but just right.

Mummy bags are fitted to the human shape. They hold the camper, and her body heat, tight like a mummy. They are usually the choice of backpack campers since those sacks tend to be lighter weight than rectangular ones. Both rectangular and mummy bags can be found in youth, adult, and tall-adult sizes.

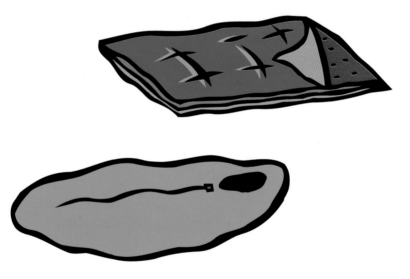

Check the tag on your sleep sack for its temperature rating. It will be a number with a degree symbol. If the number is 0 degrees, the bag will keep you warm as long as the temperature doesn't dip below 0 degrees. If most of your camping will be done during the summer or on a tropical beach, that bag may be too warm. One with a temperature rating of 35 degrees may be a better choice. Mountain campers need warmer bags (with lower temperature ratings) for cold, high-altitude nights.

Look also at what material fills your bag. Those filled with goose down are toasty warm, lightweight, and more expensive than others. Some synthetic fillings such as polyester, Polarguard, and Thinsulate are also warm but cost less and are easier to wash.

When buying a sleeping bag, check for these features:

- washability
- durable shell
- drawstring around the top to help keep your body heat in
- fabric layer inside the zipper
- temperature rating that suits the type of camping you plan to do
- filling that keeps you warm and fits your budget

CRAFTY CAMPER: BLANKET BAG

Until you purchase a sleep sack, make one.

1. Start with two blankets.
2. Place left half of one blanket over right half of the other.
3. Fold left half of bottom blanket over the two blanket layers you already have and then the right half of the last blanket over the stack.
4. Carefully pin with large safety or blanket pins.
5. Now fold up one end and pin it.
6. Crawl in and sleep snug as a skunk in a woodpile.

Sleeping Pads

Sleeping pads go under your sleeping bag, providing a layer between you and the cold, hard, sometimes rocky ground. They keep you warmer, drier, and more comfortable. Your sleeping pad might be an inflatable air mattress or a foam pad. Some versatile pads can be folded and slipped into a fabric frame, forming a camp chair for daytime use.

Necessary Camp Stuff

These are the most important things to take on your camping trip. Store them in waterproof containers (self-sealing plastic bags work fine) where they will stay dry. Keep them where you can find them.

- matches (store them in a film canister to keep dry)
- flashlight with extra batteries
- safety pins, and needle and thread (for clothing and gear repair)
- emergency candle (in case your flashlight gets lost or broken)
- compass
- emergency whistle (Keep in your pocket, or attached to a zipper, or on a cord around your neck. Use it only to call for help.)
- first-aid kit (a waterproof bag or container filled with moist towelettes, bandages, gauze and adhesive tape, small scissors, moleskin for blistered feet, aspirin or other fever/pain reducer)
- plastic garbage bags (for collecting trash and dirty clothes, putting on a wet picnic bench, or for extra rain protection)
- nylon cord (to make a clothesline or hang food in trees)
- clothespins (to secure wet clothes and dishcloths on line to dry)
- maps
- trowel or small shovel (to dig a pit toilet and food-scrap hole)
- water jug

Use these only when your adult says it's okay:
- Pocketknife (Some pocketknives have tweezers, a screwdriver, pliers, and other handy tools in addition to several knife blades.)
- Backpacker's saw (for cutting wood when you have to)

Necessary Camp Stuff

Cooking and Eating Stuff

Guess what? There are no kitchens in the woods. You have to bring your own. But how do you know what to take, especially if you've never done much cooking in the kitchen at home? Don't panic. You can cook your food over an open fire on a stick, and all you'll need in order to eat it is a cup, plate, and eating utensils. For longer trips, you'll want a variety of foods, so you'll need more equipment. Use this handy list. Take what you need from home or buy special space-saving cooking kits at a camp store. They come in individual and group sets.

Use your camp cup to measure 1 cup (or half a camp cup for 1/2 cup). Your cereal spoon is about a teaspoon, and soup spoons are about a tablespoon.

CRAFTY CAMPER: CAMP COOK KIT

Plastic tote boxes, such as those sold as fishing tackle boxes and sewing kits, can be used to hold camp cooking gear. Store cooking utensils such as tongs, wooden spoons, and spatulas in the bottom. Small things, including matches, salt, pepper, and spices, can be kept in the top tray between the dividers. Get a tote box that you'll use just for camp gear. Don't use the smelly one your brother takes fishing.

Choose heavy-duty plastic or metal dishes rather than paper plates and cups, which can be used only once, or glass, which is breakable.

Cooking Stuff

- skillet/cooking pot
- knife, fork, spoon
- cup, plate, bowl (or nested camp set)
- pot holder or oven mitt
- safety matches (coated matches that will
     light only on the striking pad of the match box)
- wooden spoon
- spatula
- serving bowl
- strainer (to remove cooking liquid from
     spaghetti, noodles, and vegetables)
- water bottle (one for each person)
- water jug (to hold camp water supply)
- aluminum foil
- self-sealing plastic bags in a variety of sizes.
     Use for mixing foods and storing leftovers.
- camp stove (available as small, one-burner
     backpacking models or larger, two- or three-
     burner styles. You may be able to help your
     adult choose and operate this.)
- can opener
- measuring cups and spoons
- paper towels
- long-handled turner or tongs
- sharp knife
- table cover
- salt, pepper, other seasonings
- ice chest (fill with ice and this becomes
     the camp refrigerator)

Cleanup Stuff

For camp:
- dishwashing soap • plastic dishpan (this is your outdoor sink)
- dishcloth • sponge/scouring pad (for scrubbing the skillet after your dad burns the fish you caught)

For campers:
- shampoo/soap • toothbrush/toothpaste• toilet paper (many campgrounds have toilet paper in the outhouse, but the camper before you probably used the last of it) • washcloth/towel • comb/brush
- insect repellent/sunscreen • personal-hygiene items
- medications you take regularly or might need

CRAFTY CAMPER: CAMPER CLEAN-UP KIT

Make this handy apron and you won't have to juggle your toothpaste, toothbrush, brush, comb, soap, and washcloth on your way to the bath-house. They'll all be together and easy to find. Remember, the bathhouse in your campground may simply be an outhouse with a water pump outside with the only light being that from your own flashlight—or it may be a building complete with electric lights, hot and cold running water, and even showers. You'll learn how to manage no matter what the facilities.

1. Fold up the bottom of a small bath towel (or a hand towel for smaller campers) about five inches.

2. Stitch the ends and additional seams vertically along the folded section, making pockets of different widths to hold your items. You'll want your adult to help you with this. If you can't find someone to help you sew the seams, use fabric glue from a fabric shop.

3. Fold the towel in half and stitch all the way across it a half-inch away from the fold.

4. Thread a shoelace big enough to go around your waist and tie through the tube you just sewed.

5. Fill the pockets and tie on your Camper Clean-up Kit. The top half of the towel hangs over your toiletries. Use it to dry your face and hands.

Clothing Stuff

Your regular ol' clothes are ideal for camping. Camp days often start and end with a cold temperature, with a warm-up in the middle, making it hard to decide what to wear. Layering your clothes is the answer. *Layering* is wearing several pieces of lightweight clothing rather than one heavy piece. The air between the layers traps and holds your body heat, keeping you warm. As the day warms up, make like a banana and peel those layers. Add them back on as the day cools.

Summer:

underwear + T-shirt + long-sleeved shirt + sweatshirt + jacket + shorts + jeans + cap or sunhat and sunscreen

Winter:

long underwear + long-sleeved flannel shirt + sweatshirt/wool sweater + parka + long underwear + sweatpants + loose-fitting pants + gloves, warm hat, two pairs socks

Rainy weather:

Add raincoat or poncho, waterproof pants, waterproof boots.

Night wear:

Depending on the weather, fresh cotton-knit T-shirt and shorts, sweats, or thermal underwear.

Footgear:

Socks:

- Thick cotton socks keep your feet cool in hot weather and warm in cool weather.
- Thick woolly socks protect hiking feet from blisters.
- Wool socks stay warm even when wet, making them the best choice for cold weather.

Shoes:

- rubber sport sandals for water
- sneakers or hiking boots
- something easy to slip into for the midnight trip to the outhouse

RIKKI'S TIPS:

1. If you're caught in the rain without rain gear, cut a head-hole in a large garbage bag and slip it on.
2. Don't sleep in the clothes you cooked in. A passing bear could mistake you for a bacon cheeseburger.
3. Don't sleep in the clothes you spent the day in. They have absorbed your body moisture and will keep you feeling like a campersicle all night.

pLaNNiNg Your trip

Once you've decided where to camp and what equipment and clothing you need, it's time for you and the adults who will camp with you to plan the trip details.

CAUTION: Don't throw your gear in the car, ride to your destination, and think you'll find the perfect camping spot on the banks of the swimming hole. You may end up with your tent pitched ten feet from the highway, if you get a campsite at all. Only the early camp bird gets a campsite. Many campgrounds now allow campers to make reservations. Some *require* reservations or permits that you must apply for well in advance of your trip. A guide to campgrounds (available at bookstores and libraries) will give you such information and provide a phone number to call with questions.

 Firewood gathering is not allowed in many campgrounds. Take your own or see if you can buy it at the camp headquarters.

Is there a camp store where you can purchase forgotten items? If not, pack carefully. Imagine getting to camp without the chocolate bars for your s'mores. Your trip could be ruined!

 Many campers like campgrounds that are for tent campers only. They won't be kept awake by a loud recreational vehicle generator kept on to power an even louder television. Most tent campers prefer watching stars, listening to animals, singing around the campfire, and telling stories for their evening entertainment

When you know how long you'll camp, plan the meals. Try the recipes in this book (pages 33 to 41). You'll need breakfast, lunch, dinner, and snacks for each day in the woods.

Once you've chosen recipes, you can make a shopping list from the list of ingredients. Before you shop, consider how you will store your food:

Fresh meats and fish should be bought the day of the trip, kept really cold, and eaten that day or the next. Refrigerated food should be packed in a camp ice chest with ice or several large ice packs. Not all camp ice chests come with a drain, but the one you buy should have one. Otherwise, you'll have to take everything out of the chest each day when it's time to drain the water and add more ice.

Bacon, lunch meats, and other meats containing preservatives can be kept for a few days if ice is replenished daily. They should be stored in seal-  able plastic bags. Cheese, eggs, and fresh veggies can also be kept for several days.

If your trip is for more than a day or two, most of the food you pack should be the kind that can keep on a shelf for a long time. You can eat well for weeks after the ice in your ice chest has melted away with some flour, sugar, grains (such as rice and spaghetti), bread, dry breakfast cereals, canned meats and fish, fruits and vegetables, instant milk, soups, sauces, and freeze-dried camp meals. Nuts and some fruits also keep well—that includes peanut butter and raisins.

Take only pictures, leave only footprints.

selecting a campsite

If you arrive at the campground and there is just one campsite left, grab it. If you have a choice, think about these things when deciding which place to take:

The ideal campsite . . .

- is roomy enough for sleeping, cooking, sitting, and cleanup areas;
- is screened from neighboring campsites by trees and bushes;
- has a level spot free of rocks and sticks that is large enough for your tent;
- is sunny in the morning and shady in the afternoon;
- is near the restroom, but not so close that the smell or traffic are problems;
- is not in a low spot. They collect moisture, have bugs, and become puddles when it rains.

Setting Up Camp

After you have checked out the camp and dipped your feet into the stream, the first thing you will do is set up your camp home. Camp, like everything else, is better with a little organization.

Cooking Area

Cooking and cleanup won't seem like such a chore if you store everything you need near the picnic table and fire ring. The picnic table will serve as your food center. If you are using a camp stove, put it at one end of the table, making sure it is level. The ice chest can be placed on the bench beside it. While preparing the meal, your utensil caddy can be on the table so you can easily reach a knife for chopping and a spoon for mixing.

While your meal is cooking, change the picnic table from food center to dinner table. Seal and put away unused food, move the utensil caddy to the cooking center, and set the table. You'll want to locate your lantern before the sun goes down.

Before sitting down to eat, put a pot of water on the stove or over the campfire to heat. (See page 29 for how to build a campfire.) It'll be hot when it's time to wash dishes. With two plastic washtubs—one for soapy water and one for rinse water—and some elbow grease, you've got yourself a dishwasher: you! It's much more fun to wash dishes outdoors while watching chipmunks play than it is at home.

You can cool your watermelon or sealed juice in the stream, but watch it carefully—if it rains and the water rises, the campers downstream may be the ones to enjoy it.

CRAFTY CAMPER: NO-PINS CLOTHESLINE

Tie two ropes, or one really long one, around a tree. Twist the length of the ropes together. Tie the new twisted rope around another tree. Stuff the ends of your wet clothes or towels into the loops created by the twisted ropes. You can also air out your sleeping bags on the clothesline when you are sure it isn't going to rain.

Sleeping Area

The tent should be on a level spot. Just a slight incline will make you feel like you're going to slide into a heap at the bottom of the tent. Many campgrounds have a level place outlined with logs and filled with smooth dirt. If yours doesn't, get on your hands and knees and clear the area of rocks and sticks. Remember *The Princess and the Pea*? Those lumps under your bed will keep you tossing and turning all night.

When that's done, put down your ground cloth and set up your tent. Blow up air mattresses and arrange them or foam pads to suit your group. Put sleeping bags atop the mattresses or pads, and clothes where you can reach them, but not against the walls of the tent. If there is rain, it will seep through the tent walls wherever anything is touching.

You'll enjoy a battery-operated lantern to shed light on bedtime reading or game playing. Headlights— flashlights you strap to your head—are good, and fun, for reading.

Headlights (or a flashlight placed near the door) are also helpful for middle-of-the-night trips to the outhouse. Put a pair of easy-to-slip-into shoes beside the light so they can be located in the dark.

Backwoods Plumbing

Cleanup

The main ingredient to any cleanup is water. The water in most camp-grounds is treated and safe to use and to drink. If there is no piped-in water, you may have to get it from a creek or lake. You can't tell by looking that the water has harmful bacteria or teeny "bugs" in it, so boil it for five minutes. That will kill anything that could make you sick. You can also use water filters and treatment tablets that can be found in camping stores.

Camp stores also sell five-gallon collapsible plastic water jugs. Fill one with water before you leave home or with treated water in camp. Tie a rope on it and hang it from a tree branch near the edge of your camp-site. If you dangle it over a vegetated area (one covered with plant growth), you won't make mud when you use it.

Put a bar of soap in a mesh vegetable bag or an old nylon stocking and tie it onto the jug handle so it hangs down near the spout. Everything you need to wash your face and hands is right where you need it.

Take a cup and your camper cleanup kit to the area and you can brush your teeth while you're there.

Solar Shower

Camp stores sell solar showers, but you can also make your own. Practiced campers can shower and wash their hair with less than two gallons of water. You may not be that fast, but you can at least rinse off the dust. One trick is to wet your hair down and apply shampoo before you start.

Hang a dark, heavy-duty trash bag on a sturdy branch. Make sure it is in a place that gets lots of sun. Pour two gallons of water into the bag. Let the sun heat it for several hours. When your hair is lathered, poke a fork into the bottom of the bag and wash fast. Experiment with stopping the water flow momentarily by pinching the open area with your fingers or a clothespin. Warning: sometimes you have to rinse with cold water.

Toilet

If there are bathroom facilities where you are camping, use those. If not, you can urinate (pee) behind any tree or rock big enough to give you privacy. Pooping is a different story. You'll need to dig a pit toilet. Why? Feces (poop) pollutes water with germs that are harmful to everyone downstream. And it isn't pleasant to stumble onto someone else's mess in the backcountry. Properly disposing of your own body waste is just plain good "forestkeeping."

If you are going to be in an area for several days, dig a bigger toilet 20 inches across and 10 inches deep. Pile loose dirt to one side and use some of it to cover what you leave after each visit.

26

Pit toilet

You may not feel comfortable asking a forest ranger the right way to poop in the woods, so read on:

1. Using your trowel, dig a hole 6 to 8 inches deep and a little wider. Pile the loose dirt to one side. The hole should be at least 100 feet from any water or any place where rain might run off into a lake or stream below.

2. Squat over the hole and do your business.

3. Use toilet paper if you have it, leaves if you don't. Put paper in the hole unless the rules at your campsite say used toilet paper must be carried out. If so, put it in a plastic bag and seal it tight.

4. Using the trowel, cover everything with the dirt that you dug from the hole.

CRAFTY CAMPER: WEATHERPROOF TOILET-PAPER HOLDER

Seal a roll of toilet paper in a half-gallon self-sealing plastic bag. Cut a slit in the bottom of the bag and pull the loose end of the paper through it. Poke two holes, one on each side of the bag, and run a 36-inch piece of string through one hole, through the toilet paper tube, and out the other hole. Tie the ends in a knot. Now this holder can be hung from a branch by your  pit toilet or around your neck where it's easy to reach when you need it. Caution: don't walk with the holder around your neck. It could get caught on a branch and choke you. (Besides, the other campers would get a good laugh at your expense.)

CAMP CHOW

One of the best parts of camping is anticipating the taste of your food while you smell it cooking over the open fire. Campers will tell you they like cookin' their grub over the campfire. They might be more accurate to say they like camp*coal* cooking. The hot, smoldering coals are what's left when the flames of your fire die down. While campfire cooking can result in marshmallow flambé, cooking over coals allows your food to be cooked more evenly.

Here are the fire rules you must follow:

1. If you see a sign like this don't build a fire at all. It's not allowed.
2. Build your fire in an established fire pit or firebox.
3. Small fires are best for cooking.
4. Stand where sparks won't blow on you. Make sure they don't blow on your tent, either.
5. Never leave the fire unattended.
6. Always have a bucket of water or sand nearby. You can use it to put out the fire if the flames get too high or the wind begins whipping it around.
7. Be sure your fire is completely out before you leave the site.

Campfires

Fire-building Materials

Even the most experienced mountaineer can't start a fire with logs. You need to start with smaller fuel. Tinder lights the kindling; kindling lights the logs.

Tinder = something small that burns easily. Small twigs, dry grass, pinecones, or crumpled newspaper are good tinder.

 Kindling = twigs and sticks slightly larger than the tinder. These are longer burning and will help light the main fuel.

Main fuel = larger logs that will burn down to hot coals that will cook your food. One log won't burn well. You'll need three or four to make the little "chimneys" that pull the fire up through the fuel.

CRAFTY CAMPER: RAINY-DAY FIREMAKERS

- Explorers waterproofed their matches by dipping them in melted paraffin (wax). Have an adult heat paraffin in an old can. When it is taken off the heat, you can drop your matches in, pull them out with tongs or a fork, and let them cool. Or, make waterproof matches by painting wooden ones with fingernail polish.
- Make "fire bugs" the same way. Roll up several sheets of newspaper tightly. Tie six-inch pieces of string around the roll every two inches. Cut through the paper halfway between the strings so you're left with many small bundles. Dip the "bugs" in the hot paraffin.

Building the Fire

Backwoodsmen know how to build different kinds of campfires for different ways of cooking. Here are some you can try.

- A tepee fire burns quickly with a lot of heat. It's good for boiling water to cook spaghetti, noodles, or vegetables.

Lay a small pile of kindling, then lean 10- to 12-inch sticks in a pyramid above it, then larger logs on top of the pyramid.

- A log cabin fire burns down to a thick bed of smoldering coals ideal for cooking feasts on a stick, in aluminum foil, or on a grill.

Lean kindling around a small pile of tinder in a tepee shape. Stack logs around the tepee like a log cabin, moving each round of logs closer to the center.

- A reflector fire is best for baking. It is built against the stone or metal wall of the fire ring. The rocks and metal give off (reflect) heat long after the fire is out.

Pile your tinder against the fire ring; lean your sticks, then your logs, over it, with one end on the ground and one against the inside of the ring.

Carefully light the tinder. Now wait patiently until the fire dies down and the coals glow red hot—about twenty to thirty minutes. Waiting is the hardest part of fire building, but when that is done, you're ready to become a smokin' campfire cook.

The Bear Facts

Take extra care if you are in country where bears live.

1. NEVER feed bears. When a bear thinks of people as a food source, she will keep coming back and become a problem bear.
2. Don't keep food inside your tent. If a bear smells your candy bar, the tent walls won't keep him out.
3. If your campground provides lockers, store your food there, or in the trunk of your car. Better yet, tie it in a bear bag—a bundle that you raise high into the trees on a rope.

No-Utensil Cooking

If you don't want to lug your whole kitchen into the bush, just take a roll of heavy-duty aluminum foil and find a good cooking stick. A good stick is sturdy and green (not dry), two-and-a-half to three feet long.

Using your pocket knife ⬤▬▬▬ , carefully shape one end into a point.

Hot dogs, sausages, marshmallows, bread dough or rolls, apples, and many other things can be cooked on the end of your stick. Make kabobs by skewering chunks of meat and vegetables onto the stick. Forked sticks are perfect for toasting bread or cooking steaks.

Wrap several layers of foil on the forked part of the branch and you've got a frying pan for cooking hamburger patties or French toast.

There are three keys to successful no-utensil, or stick, cooking:

1. Hold the food low enough over the coals to cook, but not so low that it burns. Turn often.
2. Hold the food low enough over the coals to cook, but not so low that it burns. Turn often.
3. Hold the food low enough over the coals to cook, but not so low that it burns. Turn often.

Get it? Don't be surprised if your food is charred at first. It takes practice. Just hold the food low enough over the coals to cook, but not so low that it burns. Turn often. Keep at it and one day, you'll be the best cook in the woods.

Most foods, from meats to fruits, can be wrapped in three layers of aluminum foil with the ends folded and sealed tightly, then cooked right in the coals.

Remember, the wood smoke that follows you around and blows in your face might be annoying, but it also keeps the mosquitoes away.

Use a set of barbecue cooking utensils for camp coal cooking. They'll keep your hands a safe distance from the heat.

Recipes

Wildwood Breakfasts

BROWN BAG BREAKFAST

Stick and bag cooking   1 serving

What you need:
- 1 egg
- 1 strip of bacon
- 1 lunch-size brown paper bag

What you do:
1. Lay the bacon flat in the bottom of the bag.
2. Break the egg into the bag over the bacon.
3. Fold the top of the bag down and poke the pointed end of the cooking stick through the fold OR gather up the bag top, wrap it with cotton string, and tie it onto the stick.
4. Hold the bag over the embers for 15 minutes (not too close or it will burn) or until you hear the bacon sizzling and the egg yolk is firm.
5. Tear off the top of the bag and dig in.

BAKED BACONED BANANA

Stick cooking

What you need:
- 1/2 banana
- 1 strip bacon
- 1 soft roll

What you do:

1. Peel half a banana.
2. Push one end of the bacon strip onto your cooking stick.
3. Push banana half onto cooking stick.
4. Spiral the bacon around the banana.
5. Poke the free end of the bacon onto the cooking stick above the banana.
6. Toast over hot coals until the bacon is crisp (about 5 minutes).
7. Slip the roll around the baconed banana and slip off the stick.

Since the fire is very hot, food will cook quickly on the outside and more slowly on the inside. Ask your adult assistant to help you test to see that your meat is cooked all the way through. Partially cooked meat will give you a bellyache . . . or worse.

Outback Lunch

Most campers dowse their campfires after breakfast and have a no-cook lunch so they are free to go exploring. For something special when you're hiking, try this.

PANTS-POCKET STEW

Backpack stove cooking   serves as many as contribute

Each person carries some of the stew's ingredients in his or her pockets. When it's lunchtime, campers cut up what they brought and add it to the pot. Be sure to take a backpack stove (a small, one-burner stove), stove fuel, and a soup pot. Take water, too, if none will be available at your lunch stop.

What you need:
4 pocketfuls potatoes
1 pocketful celery & 1 pocketful onion
2 pocketfuls carrots
3 pocketfuls green beans
1 or 2 pocketfuls of whatever else you want (cabbage, rutabaga, bell pepper, etc.)

8 bouillon cubes
1 tablespoon dry seasoning (carry in a sealed plastic bag)
1 can Vienna sausages or other canned meat (optional)
Knife, pot, and water (if water is not available at your lunch stop)

What you do:
1. Fill the soup pot with one cup of water per camper.
2. Add the bouillon cubes.
3. Set the pot on top of the stove, which must be in a level place away from anything burnable. With adult help, light the stove.
4. Cut the ingredients into small chunks.*
5. When the water boils, add all the other ingredients to the pot.
6. Cook for 30 minutes.

*To save time at lunch, chop the ingredients before you leave for the day. Seal them in a plastic bag before putting them in your pocket.

MUD PUPPY

stick and foil   1 serving

What you need:

   1 soft dinner roll

   1 tablespoon refried beans

   1 strip of cheese

   1 hot dog

What you do:

1. Split the top of the roll.
2. Fill the roll with beans and cheese.
3. Wrap the filled roll in three sheets of foil and seal the ends.
4. Set the pouch in the coals for ten minutes.
5. Push the hot dog onto a cooking stick, lengthwise, and cook over the coals, turning it to cook evenly.
6. Remove the roll pouch from the coals. Open carefully.
7. Put the cooked hot dog into the hot bean-and-cheese roll.

WEASEL SPUDS

foil cooking

serving

What you need:
 I large baking potato
 I pat of butter
 Salt and pepper
 Cheese (optional)

What you do:

1. Wash one large baking potato.
2. Wrap the potato in foil.
3. Nestle it into the coals and cover with more coals.
4. Ignore it for 30 to 40 minutes, or until it's soft when you squeeze it slightly with your camp tongs.
5. Carefully fish the foil pouch out with long tongs or spear it with a stick.
6. Split the foil and potato, top with butter, salt and pepper, and grated cheese if you like, then enjoy.

WILDERNESS PEACH PIE

foil cooking

What you need:
- 1 ripe peach
- 1 tablespoon sugar
- 1/4 tablespoon cinnamon

What you do:

1. Peel peach.
2. Set it on a stack of three 12-inch square sheets of foil.
3. Mix the sugar and cinnamon and sprinkle the mixture over the peach.
4. Pull the foil up, around, and over the peach and twist ends together tightly.
5. Set in the coals for 20 minutes.
6. Pull out the pouch with tongs.
7. Open the foil carefully so the ashes don't fall in your dessert and the hot juice won't burn you. Eat with a knife and fork.

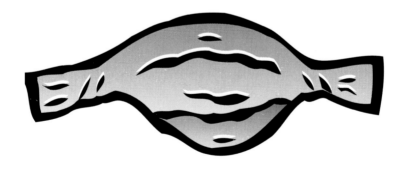

PICK-A-POCKET DINNER

foil cooking   1 serving

Cook a single meal in a small foil pocket or up to four in a bigger one.

What you need:

1 potato

1 carrot

1/4 onion

1/4 pound of hamburger

Salt and pepper

What you do:

1. Cut the potato into about 10 or 12 chunks.
2. Cut the carrot into about 10 or 12 sticks.
3. Cut the onion into small pieces.
4. Make a patty out of the hamburger.
5. Place the patty on a piece of foil, and pile all the other ingredients around it.
6. Season all with salt and pepper.
7. Wrap in foil and seal the edges.
8. Put the pocket in the hot coals and cook for 20 minutes.

Pick a different pocket next time. Try these combinations:

• Hot dog, baked beans, onion, and catsup

• Pork chop, sauerkraut, and onion

• Chicken leg or thigh, potato, celery, onion, and barbecue sauce

Or make up your own combination. Just pocket a meat, a couple of vegetables, and maybe a tablespoon of sauce, such as mustard, catsup, or soy sauce. Or leave out the meat and put in some cheese. What's your favorite?

Dutch-oven Cooking

The heavy cast-iron Dutch oven—a large pot with a lid—is a longtime favorite for camp cooking. Your food can cook for hours with only an occasional stirring in a Dutch oven while you're soaking your tootsies in a cool stream. Dutch-oven cooking can be done over a camp stove or, with a top added, snuggled into the fire's embers. You can cook most anything that you cook on the stove at home—spaghetti sauce, macaroni and cheese, scrambled eggs, etc. If your recipe has enough moisture, it'll cook for a long time with little tending.

CHILLY NIGHT CHILI

Dutch-oven cooking   4 to 6 servings

What you need:
  1 pound hamburger
  1 onion, cut into chunks
  1 stalk celery, cut into small pieces
  1/2 bell pepper, cut into chunks
  (1) 16-ounce can tomato sauce
  (1) 16-ounce can pinto beans in chili sauce

What you do:
  1. Heat the pot in the embers or over the camp stove.
  2. Put the hamburger into the pot and stir until it begins to brown.
  3. Add the onions, celery, and pepper. Cook, stirring occasionally, for 5 minutes.
  4. Stir in the tomato sauce, the beans, and half a bean can of water.
  5. Cover the pot and let cook for 30 minutes.
  6. If it becomes dry, add a little more water.

Serve with some apple slices, crackers, and chunks of cheese.

Treats

Your camp dinner isn't complete until you finish it off with this favorite camp treat!

 S'MORES

stick   1 serving

What you need:
- 1 whole graham cracker (about 2 1/2 by 5 inches)
- 1/2 flat milk chocolate bar, with or without nuts (the *whole* chocolate bar should be about the same size as the graham cracker)
- 1 marshmallow

What you do:
1. Break the graham cracker in half.
2. Place the half chocolate bar on one piece of cracker. Set aside.
3. Put marshmallow on stick. Toast it over coals until golden brown.
4. Put marshmallow on top of chocolate and cracker, and top with other graham-cracker half.
5. Press together and hold for about 30 seconds while the marshmallow melts the chocolate. Eat!

Careful—the marshmallow stays hot for a long time.

camp skills and pleasures

Your tent is pitched, your chow has been eaten and stored, and your gear is unpacked—now what? Now's the time to take advantage of being in the great outdoors. There are skills you'll need and fun things you will want to do, things that can only be done away from home. Learn them and you won't even miss the TV.

Knotty Campers

Campers use knots to make camp repairs, tie things together, and make handy camp gadgets. Using a shoelace, practice these until you can tie them quickly.

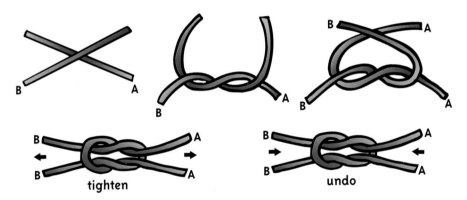

tighten   undo

Square Knot

A strong, nonslip knot that's easy to undo. Uses: Tying up bundles, such as sleeping bags; tying two ropes together.

1. Using two pieces of rope, bring the right piece (A) over and under the left piece (B).
2. Lay end B over end A.
3. Take end B under end A.
4. Pull both ropes to tighten the knot.

To undo it, simply push the rope ends toward each other.

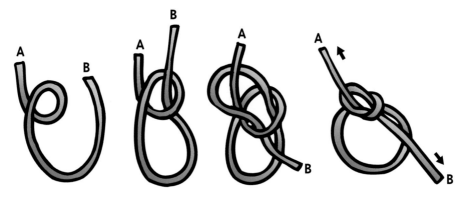

Bowline Knot

Uses: Pegging down your tent, hanging your bear bag or tarp, or docking a boat. (And you can slip the end of another rope through the knot for a lasso.)

1. Near the left end of the rope (A), make a loop the size you want it to be when finished.
2. Put right end of rope (B) through the loop.
3. Take rope end B behind rope end A, then through front of loop.
4. Pull rope A to tighten and secure the knot.

Overhand Knot

Uses: Keeping your rope from slipping back through a knot loop or tent peg hole; keeping the end of your rope from unraveling.

1. Make a loop in the string, right end (A) over left (B).
2. Take right end (A) through the back of the loop to the front of it.
3. Firmly pull both ends to tighten the knot.

Cutting-edge Safety

A good pocketknife can be a valuable tool. You'll use it many times each day to cut rope and food, and make a point on a cooking stick. A knife can be dangerous, too, if not used properly. You need to know how to open and close it, cut with it, and sharpen it. If you haven't used a knife before, ask your adult for help.

Opening the pocketknife

1. Put the end of your thumbnail into the slot on the knife blade.
2. Pull the blade up until you can grasp the blunt edge between your thumb and fingers.
3. Pull the blade out until it clicks into place.

Closing the pocketknife

1. Put the blunt edge of the knife flat against the fingers of an open hand.
2. Keeping the fingers of both hands out of the way, gently push the blade into the handle.

Cutting with the pocketknife

1. Hold the object being cut steady with one hand. Make sure your fingers are out of the way.
2. Hold the knife handle in the other hand, your thumb against the base of the blunt side of the knife.
3. Push the knife into the object being cut.
4. Always cut away from you, keeping both hands behind the knife blade.

Sharpening the pocketknife

Materials:

Whetstone (available at sporting goods and outdoor shops)

Leather belt • Knife • Oil or water

1. Put oil or water on the whetstone.
2. Place the sharp edge of the open knife against the whetstone at a slant.
3. Stroke each side of the knife blade along the stone until the edge is sharp.
4. Finish by sweeping the knife blade up and down the back side of a leather belt. This step takes off any jagged edges.

CRAFTY CAMPER: FLOAT SOAP

Practice using your knife safely by making a soap carving. Use newspaper on a flat table as a work surface.

1. Trace this fish design onto a bar of white soap.
2. Slowly and carefully cut away the large edges outside the design.
3. Carefully shape the edges of the fish with the knife blade.
4. Using the knife point, make the fish's eyes, scales, and fin details.

Nature Watch

Most people camp to be close to nature. You'll enjoy it most if you use your senses: sight, hearing, touch, smell (but not taste—more about that later). Record your findings in a notebook. Don't worry about being a great writer or artist—just capture the memory. After several camping trips, you'll start to piece together the magic of how nature works.

What do you see?

What kinds of birds, animals, and insects? What did they leave behind? Draw a picture of any bird feathers you find. Do you see animal tracks? Draw them, too. Can you tell if the maker was running, walking, or hopping? If you can't figure out who left them, you can look it up when you get home. Don't forget to look for teeth marks, too. Animals gnaw on tree bark, nut-shells, pinecones, and leaves. Sketch anything unique: hollow trees, rabbit holes, spider webs, and scratches on tree trunks you find.

What do you feel?

Take off your shoes and squish the mud between your toes. Draw that. Feel the bark of different trees. Put your paper against the bark and gently rub back and forth across it with the side of your pencil or crayon. Make rubbings of smooth bark and rough bark. Are they cool or warm? Do some have moss on them? How does that feel? Is it dry or moist? Does it grow all around the tree or just on one side? Look at the other trees in the area. Is the moss growing on the same side? Why? Catch a salamander. Hold it for a moment. Is its slippery skin warm or cool? Put on your detective hat and see what you can discover. Ask questions. Find answers.

What do you hear?

Every animal has a different voice. Can you identify a few? Listen for frogs, coyotes, owls. Their voices are easy to identify. If you hear a bird, see if you can spot it. Then you can match the sound to the bird. You'll amaze your friends when you can identify a bird after hearing its call. And it's not just animals that make sounds. Listen to the babbling brook and the wind in the tree branches. Can you find the words to describe them in your notebook? If you have a tape recorder, record the sounds to enjoy them when you get home.

What do you smell?

The fresh scent of pine, the sweet smell of wildflowers, the fishy smell near the water, the moldy smell on decaying plants in the shaded wetlands? Smells are hard to record, but keep a list of the things that you can identify. They are all part of your experience. Wood smoke from a campfire in the fall may become your very favorite scent.

What do you taste?

NOTHING! Many berries you find are poisonous. Same with mushrooms that may be deadly toadstools. The water may have nasty germs in it. The wild animals know which things are safe to eat, but you should stick to the hot dogs, s'mores, and other foods you brought from home.

The best place to look for bird and animal tracks is along the edge of a body of water. Thirsty animals go to the edge of a river, lake, or stream. The mud or sand along the bank is soft and captures prints neatly.

First Aid

Your first-aid kit contains everything you need to doctor the little cuts, bumps, and bruises that happen on every camping trip. When someone's ear is scratched by a flying fishhook, a knee is scraped by an ambushing rock, or a foot gets a blister from hiking all the way to a cave and back, you'll be able to clean the body part and ease the pain if you have the following things packed in a sealable plastic bag:

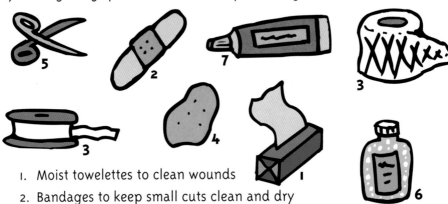

1. Moist towelettes to clean wounds
2. Bandages to keep small cuts clean and dry
3. Gauze and adhesive tape to keep larger wounds clean and dry
4. Moleskin to keep shoes from rubbing on blisters
5. Small scissors to cut gauze, tape, and moleskin
6. Aspirin or other fever and pain reducer to ease pain
7. Antibiotic cream to disinfect wounds

Your adult helper should have a first-aid kit, too, to doctor bigger hurts.

Don't forget to take and use sunscreen and insect repellent. They might keep you from having to use the first-aid kit later.

Staying Found

Being lost in the forest is no fun. There are no street signs and no familiar buildings to help you get back to camp. Not only that, but one tree can look pretty much like another.

Here are some simple things to do that will help you stay found when hiking:

- Always let someone know where you are going. • Never hike alone. • Stay on trails. • Pay attention to the land you are walking through. Occasionally turn around and look behind you so you'll know what to look for on the way back. Watch for landmarks: bent trees, oddly shaped rocks, bear caves, trees that have fallen across the stream. • Carry a whistle and a mirror. The whistle can be heard much farther than your voice can. If you flash the mirror in the sunlight, especially if you are high on a hill, it can be seen for miles and miles. • Carry an area map with you. Before setting out, sit down with your adult and look at the map. Locate roads, rivers, forests, and any landmarks you can see. Turn the map so that the markers on your map line up with what you see. Mark your campsite and the trail you are going to follow. • Always carry water and a little snack with you. You'll enjoy taking a snack break, and, if you get lost, it could make you a lot more comfortable while you wait to be found.

If you think you are lost, it is important to stay calm and stay where you are. You will be tempted to try to find your own way out, but if you are scared, you may run miles off the course. Your fellow campers will look for you in the area they think you went, so hug a tree and stay put. Blow your whistle in a series of three blows every few minutes until you are found.

If you must leave the area—for instance, in order to climb a tree or nearby hill to signal with your mirror—mark your trail so you can get back and others will know how to find you.

CRAFTY CAMPER: TRAIL MARKING

What you use to mark your trail depends on what's available. It may be grass tips tied together, stacked stones, or arranged twigs.

This symbol means "go straight ahead."

These mean "turn right."

These mean "turn left."

This means "don't go this way."

   Make sure the trail marks you make are noticeable and distinguishable from the natural surroundings.

You can make up other markings, such as a number of rocks to show how many steps to go in the direction of the marker, or one that indicates that the hiker turned around—but make sure most people can figure them out if you are really lost.

CRAFTY CAMPER: HOW LONG UNTIL SUNDOWN?

1. Hold your arm straight in front of you.
2. Put your hand out, as if you are shaking hands (thumb on top), so you can count how many fingers of sky there are between land and the sun. Remember, never look directly at the sun.
3. One finger width measures about 15 minutes, so 4 fingers means it's about an hour until the sun meets the earth.

Remember, all hands and fingers are not the same size. If your hands are small, 2 fingers may equal 15 minutes of time. Use a watch to measure it a few times until you know.

Look at Those Stars!

The number of lights you can see in the sky on a clear night away from city lights will amaze you. Most of the lights are stars—more than you could ever count. You'll also see our own moon. Some nights you can see meteors, known as falling or shooting stars. If you look hard, you may see other planets. Mars and Venus are the easiest to see. Mars appears as a small red ball. Look for Venus, the first light you see in the evening, on the western horizon. If you hear there is a comet in the sky, be sure to be

camping, for that's where you'll get the best view. Comets are rarely seen. They look like fuzzy stars with a giant tail of light.

Can you locate these constellations (groups of stars)?

URSA MAJOR (The Great Bear) • URSA MINOR (The Little Bear)
PEGASUS (The Winged Horse) • ORION (The Hunter) • LEO (The Lion)
CANIS MAJOR (The Great Dog) • CANIS MINOR (The Little Dog)
AQUARIUS (The Water Bearer)

CRAFTY CAMPER: TIN-CAN PLANETARIUM

Make your own starry night!

1. Find an empty tin can with the top removed. Be careful of any sharp edges.
2. Place the can upright on a sheet of paper and trace around the can bottom.
3. Choose your favorite constellation and draw its stars within the circle on the paper.
4. Cut out the circle, put it on the can bottom, and secure it with tape.
5. Using the awl on your knife or a nail, pierce holes at each star, through the paper and the can.
6. Put a flashlight in the open end of the can. Turn it on and shine it on your tent wall. There's your constellation—and much closer than the real one!

Some of the light we see in the night sky was created by far-off galaxies when dinosaurs walked the earth. Light travels very fast, but these places are so far away that it takes their light millions of years to reach us.

54

Singing 'Round the Ol' Campfire

When the chores are done and darkness falls, the campfire becomes the center of attention. You can be sure it won't be long until someone starts singing. Any tune you like is good for camp singing. Folk songs, cowboy songs, sea chanteys, and spirituals have long been campfire favorites. You may already know songs such as "This Old Man," "Waltzing Matilda," "Kum Ba Yah," and "A-Roving." You can find more in songbooks at the library. Here are a few wacky ones to get you started.

Underwear
(to the tune of "Over There")

Underwear, underwear,
Send a pair, send a pair, I can wear;
For I left mine lying,
Outside a-drying,
And now I need them, they're not there.
Underwear, underwear,
Get a pair, get a pair, anywhere;
The whistle's blowing,
I must be going,
For I must get there, if I have to get there bare.

Mary Had a Swarm of Bees
(to the tune of "Merrily We Roll Along")

Mary had a swarm of bees,
  Swarm of bees, swarm of bees,
Mary had a swarm of bees,
  And they to save their lives
Were forced to go where Mary went,
  Mary went, Mary went,
Were forced to go where Mary went,
  For Mary had the hives.

We May Not Be The Warmest Bunch
(to the tune of "Battle Hymn of the Republic")

We may not be the warmest bunch
   That ever hit the pike;
We may not be as handsome
   Nor as swell as you would like.
But when it comes to camping stuff,
   You'll grant that we can hike
Better than any kids in town.
   Glory, Glory, Hallelujah!
   Glory, Glory, Hallelujah!
   Glory, Glory, Hallelujah!
   His truth is marching on.

We wear our silk pajamas
   in the summer when it's hot;
We wear our flannel nighties
   In the winter when it's not.
And oft-time in the spring and fall
   We jump right in the sheets
With nothing on at all.
   Glory, Glory, Hallelujah!
   Glory, Glory, Hallelujah!
   Glory, Glory, Hallelujah!
   His truth is marching on.

Games Campers Play

Camping and games go together just like a picnic and ants. With no televisions, computers, or telephones to distract you and no schedule to keep, you'll have plenty of time to relax and enjoy playing. Generations of campers have made up games with just the materials they can find in their campground. Start by making a woods version of your favorite game.

For baseball, pitch a pinecone, dried seedpod, or whatever else is available to the batter, who will swing at it with a stick. Pinecones and seedpods can also become footballs. To play golf, use a stick club and a pinecone or small stone ball. Use a cup or can on its side for the "hole" you hit the "ball" into.

Play a game of checkers by drawing a checkerboard in the sand and using two colors of seashells or small stones for checkers. And for tic-tac-toe, make a grid in the dirt just like for checkers. Use rocks for X's and pinecones for O's, or mark them in the dirt with your stick.

Try these other games and you'll know why campers through the ages have played them:

Don't Fall in the Ocean
1 or more players

Pretend all the land is the ocean. Rocks and logs are islands. Hop from one island to another. See how far you can go before you get wet. Playing this game will improve your balance—a skill you'll use often in the woods.

Cup Toss
1 or more players

Using a stick, draw a line you will stand behind in the dirt. Take 4 giant steps forward and set several drinking cups in a line. Left to right, give each cup a number. If you have 4 cups, number them 1, 2, 3, and 4.

Stand behind your first line and toss small stones or pinecones into the cups. If you get the object in a cup, add the number of that cup to your score. The first player to reach 20 points wins.

Jump the Creek
1 or more players

Place two small sticks about 2 feet apart. Pretend the space between them is a creek. Stand behind one stick and "jump the creek." When all the players have jumped the creek, move one stick a few inches farther away. Take turns jumping. All players must be able to jump the creek before it is widened. When one player is unable to make it across, the team must work together to get that camper across. Team members hold the player's hands and, as he jumps, pull him toward the other side.

If there is a real creek where you are camping, AND YOUR ADULT SAYS IT IS OKAY, jump the real creek. On hot days, you won't mind if you don't make it across. But only jump creeks that are shallow, with slow-moving water and level bottoms.

Leaf Boat Race

2 or more players

Each player chooses a leaf or a twig to serve as a boat. Use only things you find on the ground—nothing that is growing and that you have to pick. Determine a place on the creek bank that will mark the end of the race. It might be beside a big rock or where a tree branch hangs over the water. Go upstream. One player calls out "Ready, set, go." On "go," all the players drop their boats into the stream and run to the finish line to see whose boat wins.

Remember, you must have adult approval anytime you play in the water.

Find enough twigs to play pick-up-sticks. When you've finished your game, you've already gathered the kindling for your evening campfire.

Fun After Dark

You don't have to end the fun just because the sun goes down—not if you have a flashlight.

Shadow Stories

Have you noticed the odd shadows your flashlight casts on trees and rocks at night? You can create these shadows in your tent, too, and make up stories to go with them.

All you need is a bright flashlight and your hands. Set up the flashlight to shine on a tent wall. It needs to be as far away from the wall as you are tall. Put your hands between the wall and the light and make these shapes:

OLD CAMPER • ELK • RABBIT • HORSE

If there are two people or more, each can be one of the characters. Now make up a story using the characters.

OLD CAMPER

ELK

RABBIT

HORSE

Signals in the Night

Samuel Morse invented the first way to send messages over long distances. His invention was the telegraph, which used a code—a series of dots and dashes for each letter of the alphabet. You can learn Morse Code and send secret messages past anyone who doesn't know it.

The dots are short signals and the dashes are long ones—three times as long as the dots. You can send this code by writing it, tapping it out on rocks, or flashing it with your flashlight. If the camper across the lake knows the code, he can tell you how the fishing is on that side.

When flashing, tapping, or writing a message, leave a short break between letters, a longer one between words. Here's the code:

a ._	h	o ___	v ..._
b _...	i ..	p ._.	w .__
c _._.	j .___	q __._	x _.._
d _..	k _._	r ._.	y _.__
e .	l ._..	s ...	z __..
f .._.	m __	t _	
g __.	n _.	u .._	

To end your sentence, use ._._._ for a period or ..__.. for a question mark.

When you're playing with your flashlights at night, be prepared. Sooner or later, your adult camper is going to say:

._.. .. __. .... _ ... / ___ .._ _ ._._._ /
.... .. _ / _ .... . / ... ._ __._ _._ ._._._

For privacy when you are getting ready for bed, it's best to turn off the light before you change clothes.

(Answer: Lights out. Hit the sack.)

greeN caMping

Green camping is earth-friendly camping. It means you leave little or no trace that you have camped in a place.

Old camp manuals taught campers how to dig ditches around tents so the water wouldn't run under them, to haul rocks to make a fire ring, and to cut trees to make comfy furniture. There are too many campers today to continue that way. Resources would soon be depleted if we all used whatever we pleased.

Here are some earth-friendly ways you can camp:

1. Keep a clean camp. Dispose of all waste in the campground's trash and recycle containers or pack it out.
2. Clean up any trash left by others. You shouldn't have to, but you'll be glad you did. The general rule is: "Leave it better than you found it."
3. Leave rocks, logs, dirt, or plants where they are. You came to visit nature—leave it natural.
4. Use soap and "the bathroom" far away from bodies of water. If you don't, the soap and human waste will be washed into the water with the next rain. They are harmful to the fish who live there and the animals and people who live downstream.
5. Don't have a campfire every night. The wood you use for a campfire could make a home for insects and small animals. When left to decay on the forest floor, it feeds the earth. Enjoy a campfire occasionally, but make it a special event.

Treat the forest as if it were your home. After all, it is part of it, and you'll be coming back time and again.

packing List

People new to camping, and even some longtime campers, usually take too much or too little on wilderness adventures. This list will help you decide what to take on your camping trip. Some things are essential; others may not be, depending on the type of camping you are doing. If you're camping in a motor home, you won't need a tent. If you plan to burrow into a snow cave, leave the shorts at home. After you've made a few trips, make a list that suits your own kind of camping.

Clothing Stuff

pants (short and/or long)
shirts (short and/or long)
underwear
shoes
socks
headgear
sweatshirt
coat/jacket
gloves
poncho
waterproof pants
gaiters (waterproof
  coverings for your
  lower legs)

Outdoor Stuff

matches in waterproof
  container
candles
flashlight
extra batteries
pocketknife
nylon rope (30 feet or
  more)
needle and thread

emergency whistle
compass
first-aid kit
backpacker's saw
hatchet
plastic garbage bags

Shelter Stuff

tent/ground cloth
sleeping bag
sleeping pad
pillow
tarp

Cooking Stuff

dishes/eating utensils
nested camp pots
can opener
pot holder
wooden spoons/spatula
foil
self-sealing plastic
  storage bags (various
  sizes)
food

ice chest
water bottle/water jug
camp stove
salt/pepper
water purifier

Camp Cleanup Stuff

dishwashing soap
plastic dishpans
dishcloth
sponge/scouring pad

Camper Cleanup Stuff

shampoo
toothbrush/toothpaste
soap
toilet paper
sunscreen
other personal
  items/medications
washcloth/towel
insect repellent
comb and brush

for more information

Organizations

Girl Scouts of the USA
420 Fifth Avenue
New York, NY 10018-2798
(800) 247-8319

Campfire Boys and Girls
4601 Madison Avenue
Kansas City, MO 64112-1278
(816) 756-1950

Boy Scouts of America
P. O. Box 152079
Irving, TX 75015-2079
(972) 580-2000

Outdoor Shops with Catalogues

L. L. Bean
Freeport, ME 04033
(800) 341-4341

Eddie Bauer
P. O. Box 182639
Columbus, OH 43218-2639
(800) 426-8020

R. E. I.
1700-45th Street
Sumner, WA 98390
(800) 426-4840